"TAI

MW01595322

Church
Discipline

W. H. Burnett

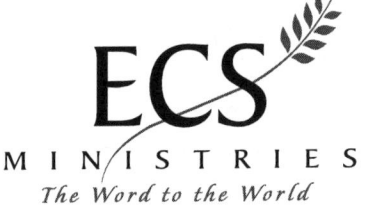

ECS
MINISTRIES
The Word to the World

Church Discipline

W. H. Burnett

Published by:
ECS Ministries
PO Box 1028
Dubuque, IA 52004-1028
phone: (563) 585-2070
email: ecsorders@ecsministries.org
website: www.ecsministries.org

First Printed 2005
Revised 2012

ISBN 978-1-59387-046-1

Code: B-CD

Printed in the United States of America

Contents

Church Discipline

W hen penning his last epistle to Timothy, the apostle Paul reminds him, *"But know this, that in the last days perilous times will come"* (2 Timothy 3:1). W. E. Vine explains in *Vine's Dictionary of Old and New Testament Words* that the word *perilous* means "hard to deal with; hard to bear; grievous."

There is no doubt that we are already experiencing the perilous times. The world we live in has become increasingly godless and sinful. Standards that were once held in honor are now swept aside by the rising tide of liberalism. And in the absence of moral standards, men do whatever they wish without restraint, while those who enforce the law stand idly by and allow it to happen or even condone the violation.

Unfortunately, this worldly attitude has also affected the church, and elders are facing many challenges as the church age draws to a close. In view of this situation, it is crucial that all members in a local assembly understand how church discipline should be applied.

The Need for Order in the Assembly

It is a well-recognized fact that no civilization can function without having laws, rules, and regulations to control the conduct of its people. In addition, it is necessary to enforce these laws for the overall good of society. The police and the judiciary deal with those who violate the law by enforcing penalties which are appropriate to the severity of the crime committed. This was the way that God dealt with Israel in the days of Moses. God gave them his Law and, if it were violated, the priests and judges would deal with the offenders.

So it is in the spiritual society called the "house of God" (1 Timothy 3:15). The New Testament epistles describe the conditions that God has prescribed to maintain order in his house. People in local church fellowship are not only partakers of the blessings that derive from this; they are also obliged to comply with the Scriptural injunctions regarding personal behavior and church conduct. Should these injunctions be violated, God has delegated responsibility to local elders—sometimes called elders, overseers, or shepherds—to administer the discipline prescribed in his Word (Hebrews 13:17).

The Problem of Ignorance

Unfortunately, the subject of discipline has been seriously neglected in the ministry of God's Word. It is not uncommon, therefore, to find people in church fellowship who have no knowledge of the various types of offence and the appropriate discipline to be applied in each case, as prescribed by Scripture. The result is that when the elders administer discipline, the grief is worsened because some in the assembly view the application of discipline as demonstrating a lack of love and forgiveness. Some might even quote, *"Judge not, that you be not judged"* (Matthew 7:1). This has divided assemblies and ruined testimonies and relationships. Another unfortunate result has been that in some cases overseers have incorrectly classified the offence and thereby applied a heavy discipline where a lighter approach should have been taken. In other cases, a light discipline has been applied where Scripture prescribes excommunication.

The Objective

The concerns mentioned above remind us of the urgent need to restate the principles associated with Scriptural discipline. While the enforcement of discipline lies in the province of its oversight, it is important that every person in the church fellowship understands what is being done and why. This booklet will address these specific topics:

1. What is the purpose of discipline?
2. What types of offence does Scripture identify?
3. What is the specific discipline associated with each case?
4. Who carries out disciplinary action in the church?
5. What are the criteria for restoration of the offender?

After these topics have been addressed we will conclude with several case studies that demonstrate the application of the principles.

The Purpose of Discipline

It should be clearly understood that, ultimately, all discipline has restoration in mind. We see this time and again in God's dealings with Israel. The book of Judges is a prime example. When Israel rejected the Lord and began worshiping the gods of other nations and practicing their pagan rituals, God allowed their enemies to overcome and oppress them. These enemies had no idea that they were instruments of God's judgment to bring about repentance and recovery among his people. But in each case, when his people repented of their sin and returned to him, God raised up a judge among them who was able to defeat the enemy and restore them to their land and their liberties.

The Babylonian captivity is another example of discipline intended to bring God's people back to himself. Among many other violations, for 490 years the nation of Israel ignored the God-given requirement that the land receive its rest every seven years (Leviticus 26:31-35). Their materialism and greed drove them to ignore this. Perhaps they thought that God had turned a blind eye to their disobedience. But after 490 years, God intervened and gave the land its rest in one long sabbatical of seventy years. He allowed Nebuchadnezzar to take his people to Babylon for that period of time (Jeremiah 25:11). However, God did not forget his people, and when the discipline had run its course, God used King Cyrus to initiate the return to Jerusalem. The discipline was over (Ezra 1:1-4).

In the New Testament, the apostle Paul deals with the serious matter of fornication in the church at Corinth. He begins by admonishing the church to *"put away from yourselves the evil person"* (1 Corinthians 5:13). However, when he writes his second epistle (after the work of repentance had been wrought in the offender's heart), he says, *"This punishment which was inflicted by the majority is sufficient for such a man, so that, on the contrary, you ought rather to forgive and comfort him, lest perhaps such a one should be swallowed up with too much sorrow. Therefore I urge you to reaffirm your love to him"* (2 Corinthians 2:6-8).

In this situation, repentance had been accomplished. Restoration is now possible. We learn that while discipline may be punitive in the first instance, it is intended to be restorative in the ultimate sense. In the same way, a surgeon takes up his scalpel and inflicts a wound which will involve pain, but his ultimate intention is the complete recovery of the person involved. So also, Scriptural discipline should be administered with deepest sorrow, in the spirit of love, and with the best interests of the church and the person concerned at heart.

The Precondition for Forgiveness

One of the principles consistently taught throughout Scripture is that there can be no forgiveness without repentance. But what is repentance? It is a change of mind which leads to a change of life. Of course, we must always maintain the spirit of forgiveness and look forward to the time when repentance is evidenced. But until that moment arrives, forgiveness cannot be exercised. Here are some examples from Scripture.

A Good Example from Joseph

When Joseph's brothers traveled to Egypt for grain, Joseph put them through several severe tests (Genesis 42-43). The reason for these tests was that he wanted to see evidence of a real change of heart before reconciling with them. Yet even during the time of testing his heart yearned for them, and he shed tears in the hope of being able to embrace them again (Genesis 42:24; 43:30; 45:2).

Indeed, they had changed in those thirteen years. When Joseph imprisoned them, he wept when he heard them say, *"We are truly guilty concerning our brother, for we saw the anguish of his soul when he pleaded with us, and we would not hear; therefore this distress has come upon us"* (Genesis 42:21-22). After this confession Joseph made himself known and embraced them with all the love of his heart. He forgave them frankly and freely.

A Bad Example from David

David's dealings with Absalom show the terrible danger of acting in forgiveness before repentance is present (2 Samuel 13-15). Absalom had murdered Amnon but had never repented. And although David understood the principles of forgiveness, Joab, his powerful commander-in-chief, pressured him. *"And the king said,*

'Let him return to his own house, but do not let him see my face.' So Absalom returned to his own house, but did not see the king's face" (2 Samuel 14:24).

A short while later we read, *". . . the king kissed Absalom"* (2 Samuel 14:33). What a fatal mistake that was! Not long afterwards we read, *"Absalom stole the hearts of the men of Israel"* (2 Samuel 15:6). With Absalom usurping David's position, David was forced to flee from before him. Such are the dangers when we violate the principle that repentance must precede forgiveness.

Examples from the New Testament

When the Lord Jesus spoke to his disciples about forgiveness, he said, *"Take heed to yourselves. If your brother sins against you, rebuke him; and if he repents, forgive him. And if he sins against you seven times in a day, and seven times in a day returns to you, saying, 'I repent,' you shall forgive him"* (Luke 17:3-4). Notice the repeated qualification of repentance.

In describing the conditions necessary for forgiveness of sin in the life of believers, the apostle John writes: *"If we confess our sins, He is faithful and just to forgive us our sins and to cleanse us from all unrighteousness"* (1 John 1:9). Repentance and confession are necessary for forgiveness of sin in the believer's life.

Scripture also teaches us to pray for the offender, even before repentance is seen, as the Lord did on the cross. (It should be noted that the leaders of Israel were acting in ignorance [which differs from an act of willful sin] Acts 3:17.) Although his tormentors had not yet repented, the Lord was praying for them (Luke 23:34). After Peter had preached on the day of Pentecost, we read, *"Now when they heard this, they were cut to the heart, and said to Peter and the rest of the apostles, 'Men and brethren, what shall we do?' Then Peter said to them, 'Repent, and let every one of you be baptized in the name of Jesus Christ for the remission of sins; and you shall receive the gift of the Holy Spirit'"* (Acts 2:37-38).

We must remember this important Scriptural principle: repentance is a precondition of forgiveness. Of course, this does not mean that we should have a harsh, bitter spirit toward the brother who has not yet repented. Indeed we should always carry the spirit of forgiveness, ready to dispense it freely when repentance is seen. But acting in forgiveness where repentance is absent is not an indication of spiritual maturity, or even of love.

Protecting the Church from Spiritual Infection

At some point in the baking of a loaf of bread, a small amount of yeast is added to the other ingredients. After the dough is kneaded, it is set aside in a warm place to rise. After thirty minutes the previously flat, dense mixture has swelled-up, sometimes beyond the top of the bowl. What happened? That small portion of yeast permeated the entire mixture and produced irreversible chemical changes.

Leaven (yeast) is often used in the New Testament as a symbol of the insidious spread of evil, whether moral or doctrinal. When allowed to fester in a church, this permeating evil will eventually affect the entire church in disastrous ways.

The Corinthian assembly is a notable example of what can happen and how it should be dealt with. Fornication of a particularly gross nature was present. A man was having an incestuous affair, presumably with his stepmother, and the church was not taking any steps against it. Already the "leaven" was at work. The apostle Paul writes, *"You are puffed up, and have not rather mourned . . ."* (1 Corinthians 5:2).

The situation required drastic action to preserve the entire church from destruction. Paul admonishes them to *"deliver such a one to Satan for the destruction of the flesh, that his spirit may be saved in the day of the Lord Jesus. Your glorying is not good. Do you not know that a little leaven leavens the whole lump? Therefore purge out the old leaven, that you may be a new lump, since you truly are unleavened. For indeed Christ, our Passover, was sacrificed for us. Therefore let us keep the feast, not with old leaven, nor with the leaven of malice and wickedness, but with the unleavened bread of sincerity and truth"* (1 Corinthians 5:5-8).

Paul again uses this same figure of speech when writing to the Galatians about the presence of doctrinal error in that assembly. He says, *"A little leaven leavens the whole lump"* (Galatians 5:9).

Thus, apart from the recovery of the person involved, godly discipline—applied in accordance with Scriptural teaching—will preserve the church from being destroyed by evil influences and activities. Elders who delay action in dealing with such matters are acting irresponsibly. Action must be immediate and specific to stop further infection.

Elders need to be sensitive to the nature of the offence and its impact on the local church. This brings us to the important area of identifying the types of offences.

Types of Offences

One of the most crucial areas of church discipline involves correctly classifying the committed offence and thereafter applying the prescribed discipline. Unfortunately, there has been a tendency to invoke the terms of Matthew 18:15-17, irrespective of the type of offence involved. This has led to unfortunate results.

MATTERS OF DISCIPLINE IN THE LOCAL CHURCH

UNPREMEDITATED	DISRUPTIVE	PERSONAL	DOMESTIC	DOCTRINAL	MORAL
A brother overtaken in any trespass (fault)	Unruly, disorderly, idle talkers, deceivers	Personal offence, brother against brother	Neglect of one's own family and household	Perverting the gospel, false teaching, refusal to submit to sound doctrine, a heretic	Sexual immorality, covetousness, idolatry, reviling, drunkenness, extortion
Gal. 6:1	1 Tim. 6:3-5 1 Thess. 5:14 2 Thess. 3:6-15 Titus 1:10-11	Mt. 18:15-17	1 Tim. 5:8	Titus 3:10-11 Gal. 1:7-9 Gal. 5:10-12	1 Cor. 5:1-13 2 Cor. 2:4-11
"Brethren, if a man is overtaken in any trespass, you who are spiritual restore such a one in a spirit of gentleness, considering yourself lest you also be tempted" (Gal. 6:1)	"Note those . . . and avoid them" (Rom 16:17) "Warn those who are unruly" (1 Thess. 5:14) "you withdraw" (2 Thess. 3:6) "Whose mouths must be stopped" (Titus 1:11) "Rebuke them sharply" (Titus 1:13)	Stage 1 Go to him and resolve it on a personal basis (Mt. 18:15) Stage 2 If unsuccessful, take 1 or 2 witnesses (Mt. 18:16) Stage 3 If this is also unsuccessful, take it to the church (Mt. 18:17) If all efforts unsuccessful . . .	"He has denied the faith and is worse than an unbeliever" (1 Tim. 5:8)	"Let him be accursed" (Gal. 1:9) "A little leaven leavens the whole lump" (Gal. 5:9) "I could wish that those who trouble you would even cut themselves off" (Gal. 5:12) "Reject a divisive man" (Titus 3:10-11)	"Deliver such a one to Satan for the destruction of the flesh" (1 Cor. 5:5) "Purge out the old leaven" (1 Cor. 5:7) "not to keep company with immoral people" (1 Cor. 5:9) "Put away . . . the evil person" (1 Cor. 5:13)

REPENTANCE — **RESTORATION** — **REPENTANCE** — **EXCOMMUNICATION**

As we will see, Matthew 18 is not intended to be a "catch-all" for each and every kind of offence, but rather is specific to offences of a particular and personal nature between brethren. *"If your brother sins against you . . ."* (v. 15). It is quite inappropriate to apply the terms of Matthew 18 to other types of offence and, in particular, to matters affecting the corporate body. At this point we will identify the various classes of offences and their prescribed disciplines.

The New Testament identifies at least six types of offences. These can be further divided into two categories:

1. Offences that can be remedied apart from excommunication.
2. Offences where excommunication is prescribed.

Offences Which Can Be Remedied Apart from Excommunication

Unpremeditated Offences: Galatians 6:1

Paul writes, *"Brethren, if a man is overtaken in any trespass, you who are spiritual restore such a one in a spirit of gentleness, considering yourself lest you also be tempted"* (Galatians 6:1).

The offence being dealt with here is not of the premeditated sort which has been perpetuated as a habit of life; rather, it is a one-time slip, made in a moment of weakness, and not repeated. The prescribed action here is *"to restore such a one . . ."* In his *Expository Dictionary,* W. E. Vine explains that the word *restore* used in the passage means "to mend, to furnish completely." Again he compares this person to "a dislocated member of the spiritual body."

In such cases the skillful hand of restoration is required. An experience in the apostle Peter's life is a prime example of this type of offence and its remedy. Peter was caught off-guard as he stood by the fire in the courtyard of the high priest's house. There he blatantly denied the Lord, even going so far as to use oaths and curses.

But, as the rooster crowed, Peter immediately knew that he had committed a terrible sin. After all his boasting about never forsaking the Lord, even unto death, Peter denied the Lord at his most vulnerable hour. No one needed to sit down with Peter and explain the need for repentance. Rather, we read, *"So Peter went out and wept bitterly"* (Luke 22:62). The disciple was ashamed of what he had done, and grief filled his soul.

What spiritual future would there be for a man like this? It would appear that he had ruined his testimony and opportunity for service. Who would use a man who had not only denied the Lord but had also cursed to emphasize his point? In the depression and discouragement that followed, Peter reverted to his former life of fishing. It was here that the Lord intervened. In a spirit of com-passion, the Lord tenderly restored him and recommiss-ioned him to become one of the prominent apostles in the early church (John 21:15-19; Acts 2:14-47).

Note that the apostle Paul specifies that the people undertaking the work of recovery must be spiritual men (Galatians 6:1). These men of discernment must understand how to balance firmness with tenderness. They must be able to restore the offender without depreciating the seriousness of the committed offence.

Disruptive Offences: 1 Timothy 6:3-5; 1 Thessalonians 5:14; 2 Thessalonians 3:6-15; Titus 1:10-11

These are the "nuisance" types of offence; the kind that plague assemblies and cause heartache to elders and church leaders—the unruly, the disorderly, the vain talkers, the deceivers.

It would appear that the main characteristic of these people is that they speak carelessly and rashly and thereby create disorder and confusion among God's people. Paul indicates that such people must be dealt with in a prompt and decisive manner, as their behavior can easily disrupt the unity and peace of the entire assembly. The elders have a number of options available to them in dealing with such offences, including warning, social avoidance, and public rebuke. The approach taken will depend on the severity of the case being dealt with.

In this case, the offence has not yet reached the point where excommunication is prescribed; rather, the previous disciplinary steps must be enforced with the intent that such a brother or sister will repent and be restored.

If a disruptive offence is persisted in after being admonished, it could be classified as "reviling." Referring to the chart, reviling is listed under "Moral Offences" (see page 17). In 1 Corinthians 5, the apostle Paul groups together several offences deserving of excommunication. Reviling is one such offence (vv. 9-11). In his *Believer's Bible Commentary,* William MacDonald writes:

> "To the list of sinners mentioned in verse 10, Paul adds revilers and drunkards in verse 11. A **reviler** is a man who uses strong, intemperate language against another. But we would add a word of caution here. Should a man be excommunicated from the church if on one occasion only

he should lose his temper and use unguarded words? We would think not, but would suggest that this expression refers to a habitual practice. In other words, a **reviler** would be one who is known as being characteristically abusive toward others."

Personal Offences: Matthew 18:15-17

Here the offence is of a personal nature between two parties—*"If your brother sins against you"* (v. 15). This is perhaps the most prevalent type of offence in assemblies. Most assembly troubles do not involve important doctrinal or moral issues, but rather petty personality clashes that disrupt the peace and the unity of the assembly and grieve the heart of the Lord.

Stage 1

In this case, the technique is to keep the matter to as small a circle as possible. The offended person is told *"Go and tell him his fault between you and him alone"* (v. 15). Unfortunately, the natural tendency is to immediately tell the matter to others, with the goal of gathering support. When this is done, the church aligns itself with each of the people involved and corporate unity is destroyed. No! says the Lord—*"between you and him alone."*

It takes humility for one brother to go to the other, not only to tell him of his fault, but also to confess what part he might have had in provoking this reaction. Complete transparency is vital at this stage if the matter is to be settled amicably. And if this approach is successful then the matter can be put to rest without involving other believers or church leaders. Again, this approach pertains only when dealing with personal issues between believers.

Stage 2

If the personal approach described above is unsuccessful, the offended brother is advised to take one or two believers with him as witnesses and to make a second attempt at reconciliation (v. 16).

This should warn the offender that the situation is growing more serious, as the purpose of having others involved is that *"every word may be established"* (v. 16). This anticipates further, more drastic action, where the witnesses will speak before the church to verify the facts of the interview if this second approach is unsuccessful. The hope and intended goal is to see repentance and reconciliation without the need for further corporate action (see below).

Offences Where Excommunication Is Prescribed

Stage 3

Should matters proceed beyond the second attempt at reconciliation, the matter is to be brought to the church. This is the highest level to which an issue can be elevated. The church body must now make a ruling on the matter. Notice that even at this stage there is the possibility that corporate action can be avoided. We read, *"If he refuses even to hear the church . . ."* (v. 17). This infers that he has a last opportunity to do so, and if even at this late hour he submits to the church, he can be restored on the basis of his repentance. If, however, he refuses to hear the church, he is to be excommunicated. The Lord says, *"Let him be to you like a heathen and a tax collector."*

Domestic Offence: 1 Timothy 5:8

This issue of concern deals with domestic ir-responsibility and neglect, where a believer may fail to provide the basic necessities of life for his family. Clearly this does not address conditions of hardship where a brother lacks the resources or the opportunity to support himself or his family. In such a case, the church is responsible to provide assistance.

The condition being described here is where a brother has the ability and the opportunity to provide for his family, but he lacks the will to do so. He prefers a life of indolence and ease. This is viewed as one of the serious offences demanding excommunication. Paul writes, *"He has denied the faith and is worse than an unbeliever."*

Doctrinal Offences: Galatians 1:7-9; 5:10-12; 2 Timothy 4:2-5; Titus 3:10-11

Doctrine is absolutely fundamental to the faith. It is the bedrock on which all else rests—hence the need to act immediately should any attempt be made to pervert or undermine it. As believers we cannot tolerate any distortion of the foundation on which the church is built. This requires prompt and powerful action to stop the error before the church is destabilized. Regarding the definition of false doctrine, Scripture identifies four main aspects: perverting the gospel, false teaching, refusing to submit to sound doctrine, and heresy.

Dealing with False Doctrine

The difficulty here is determining under what circumstances the label "doctrinal error" should be applied. Since this is a serious charge, it is suggested that the following tests be applied before proceeding:

1. Determine whether the teaching involved concerns fundamental truth or peripheral matters.

It must be recognized that there are certain areas where differences of opinion in biblical interpretation are permissible. Other times, differences are not acceptable.

For example, if a brother holds a different view on eschatology than is popularly accepted, we might not wish to have him teach it in our church. But we cannot label opinioned differences on prophetic interpretation as doctrinal error. However there are matters where differences cannot be tolerated. Several examples of fundamental, non-negotiable doctrinal issues include:

- ✓ The eternal Sonship of Christ
- ✓ The deity of Christ
- ✓ His humanity
- ✓ His sinlessness and impeccability
- ✓ His atoning death, burial, and resurrection
- ✓ His ascension to the Father's right hand
- ✓ The doctrine of salvation through faith, apart from works

These issues are all foundational to the faith; there cannot be compromise on such matters. Doctrinal error in these areas demands the extreme action of excommun-ication. In short, the necessary stance to take on doctrinal issues is:

- ➢ On Fundamentals . . . immovable (Galatians 1 & 2)
- ➢ On Peripherals . . . flexible (Romans 14:1-15:7)
- 2. If the teaching is clearly false doctrine, determine whether the person is acting in ignorance or whether he has fully embraced the falsehood.

If the person involved is acting or teaching in ignor-ance, church leaders must attempt to remedy the situation through corrective teaching. If this is successful, no further action is required. If, however, the person fails to accept remedial teaching and is shown to be entrenched in doctrinal error, he must be excommunicated before this "leaven" affects the entire church body.

Dealing with an alleged case of doctrinal error is a serious matter demanding discernment and wisdom. This is the reason why an elder must be *". . . able to teach"* (1 Timothy 3:2). An elder must be able to use Scripture to identify and refute false doctrine. Otherwise the flock will be susceptible to attack from the grievous wolves without and to those speaking perverse things within (Acts 20:29-30).

Dealing with Those Who Hold False Doctrine: Revelation 2:14-15

In Revelation 2, the church at Pergamos was rebuked for having those who "held" false doctrine. The Lord says, *"I have a few things against you, because you have there those who hold the doctrine of Balaam . . . Thus you also have those who hold the doctrine of the Nicolaitans, which thing I hate."* From this it appears that if someone holds false doctrine, discipline is required, even if he is not actively teaching that false doctrine.

These verses in Revelation 2 make it clear that a church must take proactive steps to deal with false doctrine to prevent subsequent damage to the church. To take no action because the leaven is lying dormant is a false premise of love and forgiveness. The leaven must be rooted out before it creates damage. And yet, we must remember that this action is to be done in a spirit of genuine love and compassion.

Moral Offences: 1 Corinthians 5:1-13; 2 Corinthians 2:4-11

The above passages list offences serious enough to warrant excommunication. These are fornication, covetousness, idolatry, reviling, drunkenness, and extortion. The above list is intended to be typical only, and the fact that an offence is not specifically listed does not mean that no action is necessary. For example, murder is not included, but it would clearly qualify for excommun-ication. Elders are required to exercise discernment when identifying moral issues. In the case of moral offence, the action is clear: putting away and denial of social contact until the discipline has run its course and the person has been restored to fellowship.

The Application of Discipline

If an offence requires public church discipline, the question that must now be addressed is, "Who should exercise the discipline?" The apostle Paul gives direction on this matter. *"In the name of our Lord Jesus Christ, when you are gathered together, along with my spirit, with the power of our Lord Jesus Christ"* (1 Corinthians 5:4). Here Paul anticipates that the enforcement of discipline will be an action of the church, and not only the action of the elders. This is further endorsed when he refers to the disciplinary action in Corinth as having been *"inflicted by the majority"* (2 Corinthians 2:6). It was a corporate action of the entire church.

It is the church that receives people initially, excommunicates offenders, then restores and receives offenders back into local fellowship. The overseers in the church would typically present the case to the church body, with the prescribed discipline, for the affirmation of the church. Similarly, when repentance and reconciliation have been achieved, the offending party should be publicly received back into fellowship in the same manner as a new applicant / member would be announced and received.

The Problem of Litigation

Another factor of important consideration is the question of litigation. Every time elders enforce discipline, they become susceptible to lawsuits brought by people unfamiliar with church discipline or people unwilling to submit to the discipline. This can cause elders considerable anguish, especially when they face the possibility of extended legal action. The subsequent fall-out could not only destroy the church, but also bring financial ruin and consequences to family, career, and character.

This booklet does not offer legal advice on such matters, but suffice to say that nothing must be allowed to impede the sacred obligation that elders have to proceed with what Scripture prescribes.

In the end, elders must act in accordance with Scripture and leave the consequences, legal or otherwise, with the Lord. We cannot allow fear of consequences to undermine the Scriptural principles associated with church discipline.

A Final Note

We have all heard of cases where—to avoid the possibility of litigation—the elders have asked the offender to voluntarily withdraw from the fellowship rather than be "put away." Thereafter an announcement is made, advising the church of the offender's "withdrawal."

While we sympathize with the difficult situations that elders encounter, asking the offender to withdraw does not fulfill the Scriptural command to excommunicate. The offender must not be allowed to decide what is to be done, whether or not he will withdraw, and when or if he may return. This authority belongs exclusively to the elders and is something for which they alone are accountable. The offender must be put away and the consequences left with the Lord.

Summary

For its spiritual health and vitality, discipline must be conducted by the local church. Despite the liberal standards adopted in the secular world, the church must maintain the standards set by God in his Word.

When discipline is required, it is critical that overseers should first correctly classify the offence. It is here that things often go wrong; the offence is either exaggerated or trivialized, and wrong measures are applied. Too often a severe discipline has been enforced where Scripture prescribes a lesser form. In other cases, a serious offence has been trivialized by discipline too light for the matter.

Finally, discipline must never be exercised in a vindictive way; rather, it should be administered with sorrow of heart and longings that the offender should eventually be restored through repentance and recon-ciliation.

Case Studies

While this booklet provides the Scriptural basis for church discipline, the greatest difficulties arise when attempting to implement these principles in the day-to-day matters of church life. With this in mind, the following three hypothetical cases may give insight into the application and implementation of the principles involved.

Case Study 1

Problem

A young couple, engaged to be married, approach their church elders. They are distraught and confess that, on one single occasion, they allowed their emotions to overcome their better judgment. They consequently engaged in sexual activity. They confirm that this has not continued; it was one single act of indiscretion. Not only do they recognize that their conduct was wrong and make no excuses for it, but they also submit themselves to the elders for these men to determine appropriate disciplinary action.

Discussion

First, the elders must decide which category this offence comes under (refer to chart). Being of a sexual nature, it will either come under the category "Unpremeditated Offence" (Galatians 6:1) or "Moral Offence" (1 Corinthians 5:1, 13). Clearly the current case bears no resemblance to the Corinthian example, for the following reasons:

1. The sin at Corinth was being perpetuated as a habit of life. In contrast, this young couple had indulged only this once.

2. The Corinthian situation involved gross sin where a stepson was having relations with his stepmother. In contrast, this couple was already engaged to be married in an honorable way.

3. The Corinthian offender was acting in a cavalier manner and strutting his sin publicly. In contrast, this couple was distressed about their sin and prepared to accept whatever discipline the elders thought appropriate.

Classification of the Offence

Taking all things into consideration, this situation should come under the category "Unpremeditated Offence." Excommunication in this case would be entirely inappropriate and harmful to the future of those involved. The issue is not so much that what they did was wrong, but when they did it, since marriage was shortly to take place.

Action Required

Next, what disciplinary action should be taken to send the right message regarding standards to be maintained in the church, while at the same time encouraging the young couple to be restored? In a similar situation known to the author, elders decided to ask the young couple to abstain from attending the Lord's Supper for a one-month period. Additionally, an announcement was made to the church body advising them of what had happened and how the elders had come to the conclusion to deal with the matter in this way. The young couple was later restored and the assembly was preserved.

Comments

The decisions taken by the elders in this case were entirely correct. They properly classified the offence as an "Unpremeditated Offence." They also recognized that some form of discipline was required to make others aware of the seriousness of the offence and that this conduct could not be tolerated. A recent article on church discipline identified two objectives (found in 1 Timothy 5:20) that must be met in addition to dealing with the offender. These were:

- ✓ To set an example for the rest of the body.
- ✓ To promote godly fear in the rest of the flock as a warning against sin.

Case Study 2

Problem

A woman is saved at a gospel meeting held in a local assembly. She has been through an abusive marriage, was later abandoned, and is now divorced. Her husband has remarried and has had children with his second wife. The woman requests to be baptized and later applies to join the fellowship of the local church. At this stage problems arise when several members become vocal in their determination that she not be allowed to join their fellowship. They even go so far as to insist that they will leave if this woman is indeed allowed to join their church.

Discussion

Many who now come to Christ under the preaching of the gospel have been through the heartache of abuse, abandonment, divorce, etc.

Their homes and hearts have been broken and their marriages are in disarray. In coming to Christ, they find forgiveness, cleansing, healing, acceptance, and a Friend who will never leave them nor forsake them (1 John 1:7; Hebrews 13:5-6). However, in many cases, fellow Christians abandon them because of some discovery about their past. This attitude completely denies the spirit of Christ and is contrary to the Christian principles of love and compassion (Luke 10:30-37).

Although we all hate divorce and its consequences, we cannot isolate this sin from other sins. Christ has forgiven us of so much. We in turn must likewise forgive one another and enjoy the fellowship that we have in Christ. We should remember the story of the healing of the man born blind (John 9:1-38). Despite the miracle that had taken place, the Pharisees insisted on bringing up his pre-conversion status saying, *"You were completely born in sins . . . and they cast him out."* It was then the Lord met him, because he also was an outsider. Again, in dealing with the woman caught in the act of adultery, Jesus said to her, *"Neither do I condemn you; go and sin no more"* (John 8:11). Similarly, this should be our response to the situation under consideration.

Action Required

Because this woman's divorce occurred while outside of Christ and outside of church fellowship, she should not be subjected to church discipline. Christ has cleansed and freed her from her sins. Clearly there is no Scriptural impediment to her coming into fellowship.

Comments

Regarding those who threatened to leave the church and pressured the elders to deny the woman church fellowship, elders cannot allow threats, veiled or otherwise, to affect their decisions. Any attempt to do so must be dealt with as a "Disruptive Offence" (refer to chart).

Case Study 3

Problem

A brother teaches that infant baptism is an acceptable alternative to believer's baptism as taught in the New Testament. He does not believe that such people need to be baptized again when they become believers. His beliefs have been derived from typical teaching in the Old Testament rather than from the clear instructions of the New Testament. People influenced by this brother's teaching expect full fellowship in the local church without ever being baptized as believers.

Discussion

Although typology (the study or systematic classi-fication of types) has its place in illustrating New Testament doctrine, the pattern and practices of the New Testament church must not be derived from convoluted thinking involving Old Testament types.

In the Great Commission, the Lord specified, *"Go therefore and make disciples of all nations, baptizing them in the name of the Father and of the Son and of the Holy Spirit . . ."* (Matthew 28:19). Baptism followed becoming a disciple. From the book of Acts, we learn that believer's baptism played a vital role in the early church. This act of identification with Christ followed immediately after profession of salvation. Those who had previously been baptized by John had to be rebaptized in the name of the Lord Jesus (Acts 19:1-5). There is not a single instance of an unbaptized believer in the entire New Testament except for the dying thief on the cross, who obviously did not have the opportunity.

Classification of the Offence

Clearly, the offence involved is of a doctrinal nature and, as such, could destabilize the church if allowed to continue. It is a "leaven" that must be purged out before the whole is affected.

Action to Be Taken

The steps previously outlined in the section dealing with Doctrinal Offences should be followed:

1. Elders should meet with the brother and evaluate whether he is ignorant of the truth involved. If this is indeed the case, remedial teaching should be given. If he responds and repents, no further action is required against him. However, because the church has been affected, the elders must make a public announcement outlining the problem, describing what has been done about it and indicating that special teaching sessions will be conducted immediately to clarify the New Test-ament teaching.

2. If the elders meet with the brother and he demon-strates an unwillingness to forsake his doctrinal position, further disciplinary action must be taken to preserve the assembly and to hopefully bring about repentance and restoration. In a situation like this, the elders are required to "put him away," as the false teaching will fester if allowed to continue.

Comments

Some people might suggest that the brother should be silenced in the assembly meetings and that this would suffice, provided he agrees not to teach this error in the future. This is not an acceptable way of dealing with doctrinal error. The leaders of the church at Pergamos were rebuked for allowing those who "held" false doctrine to remain in fellowship (Revelation 2:14-15).

Discussion Questions

1. What is the difference between what Jesus taught in Matthew 7:1-6 and what He said in Matthew 18:17-18 about offenses?

2. Does Romans 14 and 15 apply? Why or why not?

3. Why is church discipline so important and what is the purpose of it?

4. What must take place before there can be forgiveness for an offense from God and others?

5. How can we express forgiveness before the conditions are met?

6. What six different types of offenses are there and into what two categories can they be classified?

7. What offenses might be considered personal and what is the first step towards restoration in this case? How might this be preventative of more serious offenses?

8. How are disruptive offenses to be dealt with?

9. For what offenses would a person be ex-communicated from the church for and who exercises this discipline?

10. Explain the process of dealing with an offense from the first step to the last. Take into consideration all types of offenses.

Finally, we all need to carefully examine our own hearts knowing that each of us has likely been guilty of one of these offenses at some point in our lives, whether it be unpremeditated, personal, moral, etc. Let us seek forgiveness from our Lord and ask His protection from engaging in those offenses in the future. For by so doing we hinder the work of the Lord both in our lives and in the local assembly.